The Adventures of Quentin and Gracie

Japan

By Emily Logan

Printed in the United States of America
First Edition, 2020

This book is dedicated to Katherine, Noah and Amelia Jones for so graciously hosting us while we explored the beautiful country of Japan with you. Thank you for being part of our tribe! We love you!

A second dedication goes out to Yuriko Takeuchi for always taking such good care of me when I am in Japan. Thank you for being the best 'Japanese mama' a girl could ever ask for :)

Konnichiwa (hello) from Japan or Nippon as the locals call it! This country's nickname is the 'land of the rising sun' because the sun comes up really early in the morning.

Japan is a country that is made up of many islands but has 5 main islands. It is located in the Pacific Ocean and is part of the Asian continent.

Come join us as we explore this ancient culture!

After we got settled from the long flight, we went to a sushi restaurant where the food passes you on a moving belt. When you see something that you want to eat, you just grab it and enjoy!

Do you know how to use chop sticks?

After finishing our meals, we headed to do some karaoke. We had our own little room to sing in. We felt like superstars!

The next morning we explored Tokyo, the capital and largest city in the country. We ended up at a place called teamLab: Borderless where you are 'a part of the art' as soon as you step inside. This is one of the neatest places I have ever been to in my whole life!

In our favorite room, Gracie and I colored pictures of fish and reptiles, then put them in a machine that made them come to life! We chased our creations all around the room as they swam and crawled on the floor and walls!

The next day we took a trip to Kamakura to check out the sights over there. We noticed something that looked like a big bathtub. This is a place where people wash their hands off to show respect before they visit a shrine.

When we walked in the gates, we saw the biggest Buddha that I had ever seen in my life! Even his sandals that were hanging on the wall were bigger than me!

Mount Fuji is the biggest volcano in Japan and the second biggest in the world. You can hike all the way up to the top. Many people who go up for the first time, get a hiking stick that they get stamped at each station to show how far up they went.

Getting to the summit (top) is very difficult. Did you know that the summit is so high up, even the weather can be different up there?! It is higher than the clouds so it can feel like winter at the top even though it is summer at the base.

We went to the yunessun (hot spring) the next day. Japan has many, but my mom's favorite is in Hakone. They had water slides, pools and even a waterfall. They have relaxing baths filled with things like coffee, green tea, wine and rose petals.
If you could swim in anything, what would it be?

There was a foot bath that was filled with little fish who cleaned people's feet. As soon as we stuck our feet in, they came right over to us. They swam in between our toes and we laughed so hard because it tickled so much! Are your feet ticklish?

Most people in Japan use trains to get around instead of cars. At first, we were nervous because of how crowded it was but it turned out to be just another fun adventure. We took the Shinkansen bullet train to Kyoto. It goes almost 200 miles per hour!

In any culture it is important to be polite, but in Japan it is expected. If you see a person that is older, or just looks like they need to sit down, you should get up and give them your seat.
I love how kind Japanese people are!

When we first arrived in Kyoto, we explored on a rickshaw. At the top of the hill, we saw magnificent pagodas and even drank from the Kiyomizu Temple fountain of youth for good luck.

At the shrines, there are places for people to make a wish or pray if they want. Some places have candles or incense to light and little wooden prayer requests to hang up.

My mom's favorite statue in Kyoto was Ryozen Kannon. It is the only female 'Giant Buddha' and was built to remember all of the Soldiers from World War 2.

Our last stop while in Kyoto was the famous Fushimi Inari Shrine. That place was so cool! There were thousands of Toriis lined up in a row. The path stretched for over 2.5 miles.

Our next journey took us to Hiroshima. We visited the Peace Park Memorial and Museum. Seeing the destruction that the atomic bomb caused was really sad but my mom said that it's important to learn about history so it doesn't happen again. Hiroshima is a good reminder that it is so important to be nice to others.

At the children's memorial, we saw thousands of paper cranes sent in by people from all over the world.

Do you know how to fold a paper crane?

Miyajima is a super fun island where wild deer walk around with people. We walked down the waterfront path that was lined with super cool shrines. At the end there is a beautiful temple and a huge Torii gate that looks like it is floating in the water.

After that, we took a cable car up the steep mountain where we got to see the water all around us-there were even some monkeys in the trees!

When we returned back up to the Tokyo area, we visited a couple of interesting cities, first was Shinjuku. The train station there is one of the largest in the country -more than 3.6 million people pass through that station every single day!

I was so surprised to see that Japan has both Tokyo Disney and Disney Sea! My sister loved Ariel's underground play area and I loved all of the rides. What is your favorite Disney movie?

One day, my mom and sister dressed up in kimono and I dressed as a samurai. There are so many layers to the kimono that two people had to help them get dressed.

Kimonos are elegant traditional clothes that Japanese people used to wear. They now mostly wear them for special occasions but we still saw many people walking around in them during our trip.

There are more than 77,000 temples in Japan and the oldest one is over 1,400 years old.

My favorite is the Nijo Castle which is known for it's 'Nightingale Floors'. They were built with nails under the boards so every time you take a step, the floor squeaks or 'chirps' like a bird. This is like a home alarm system. I bet even the ninjas couldn't get past that floor! Can you walk as quiet as a ninja?

We visited a temple called the Golden Pavilion. It is painted with REAL gold and when you look at it from far away, it looks like there are two of them because you can see it's reflection in the water.

Sports are very popular in Japan. We went to a baseball game and watched sumo! Sumo is a sport where two large men try to push one another out of a big circle. Even though we couldn't understand what they were saying, it was so much fun to watch the games and cheer with the crowd!

Did you see our friend Yuki the lucky baby Buddha on each page? If not, go back and look for him. On some pages he is hanging out with us but on other pages he's hiding pretty well.

Can you say these Japanese words?

Konnichiwa (hello)-- Koh-nee-chee-wah

Ohayo Gozaimasu (Good Morning)-- Ohio (like the state)
Goh-Zai-Mas

Hai (Yes)-- Hi

Iie (No)-- Eee-ay or No ('No' is used a lot and is understood)

O-negai shimasu (please)-- Oh-Ne-Guy-She-Mas

Domo Arigato (Thank you)-- Doh-Moh Ah-Di-Gah-Tow

Sumimasen (Excuse Me)-- Soo-Me-Mah-Sehn

Wakarimasen (I don't understand)-- Wah-Kah-Dee-Mas-En

Japan is an ancient culture with many customs that we may not be used to. It is always best to do your research so you don't offend anyone when you go places. Some customs to be aware of to make your adventure more polite are:

* When riding an escalator, stand on the left and pass on the right

* Do not wear shoes in the house (and many restaurants)

* Tell your parents no tipping when you go out to eat

* Don't stick your chopsticks straight (up and down) into your rice

* Don't talk on the phone when on a train

Word Search

B Y P

T N Q N P V R S M

W H R D U Q R T F R G W N

G S F I X V U T K A H H H S J I I

M A Z C Y P P U U O Z Y N J U Y K A Q

H S D R G G T E I C E X V T E M M W B R W

K O P Z E V D I I K S E E Q S O S D A I T

E W Y I Y P E J B V I V D Q W G L R N C B R W

N U V W D U U Z J P M V B W Z C Q I V V A A I

E I L J D B F V T Y V O L X Z T R Z W G W B Y J G

Q R M W G U D X S E B N R O I R S Q M X W Q C C F

Q H A L H E U X I N N O S E A G B V Y B B Y U M C

K N S H C M N Y J U I X O Y K O T G I A U G I Y G H F

G D R I T M M P G N B Y M M O J Y J G T L Z U Z Z J M

D P B Q S G V L U C W M X T A B Q W V A L Z A S K F I

K X P I U N H C C K A M H R E W O M J E X P B X H

O W N S K T U R N T K V T A X R Q H X T O T F S S

P D I O R D X Q Z A J E X K S I X Y U V L W U R J

X Y R P G H X N Z M D W I G Z O T N I H S O D

U T X P P U J Z A B I U B U D D H A B S A G N

E Q D Q I A P E P Q F A S A C T E J C K C

D Z K I L N W A B A U Z K A R I I R O T R

H V H M N J T G P J S B I A Q K A G W

R G P W D V N O O H I H N K S P V

W V H H Z L D E Q R E I A

J K I D A A I Z A

M W N

Asia
Buddha
Bullet Train
Crane
Fuji

Japan
Kanji
Karaoke
Kimono
Nippon

Pagoda
Shinto
Shrine
Sumo

Sushi
Tokyo
Torii
Yen

Also check out:

Adventures of Quentin and Gracie-Oahu, Hawaii

Keep up with us at:

AdventuresOfQuentinAndGracie

and

www.loganfamilyllc.com

www.ingramcontent.com/pod-product-compliance
Lightning Source LLC
LaVergne TN
LVHW070157110826
845147LV00002B/434